Series 561

THE STORY OF
CHARLES II

by L. DU GARDE PEACH,
M.A., Ph.D., D.Litt.

with illustrations
by JOHN KENNEY

Publishers : Wills & Hepworth Ltd., Loughborough

First published 1960   ©   *Printed in England*

THE STORY OF CHARLES II

When a King of England dies, the next in succession to the Throne becomes at once the reigning Sovereign. This is what we mean when we say, "The King is dead: long live the King".

When King Charles the First was executed in 1649, his son became King Charles the Second.

Although he was the rightful King of England, Charles II was not in a position to rule the country. In the Civil War between his father, King Charles I, and the Parliament, the King had been defeated and England was governed by a body of men known as Puritans, whose leader was named Oliver Cromwell.

Charles II fled first to France and then to Scotland where, as the grandson of the Scottish King James VI, he was crowned. He was now King of Scotland, but his intention was to return to England with an army of Scottish soldiers, and to regain the English Throne which his father had lost.

Oliver Cromwell knew that Charles was preparing an army to invade England. In order to prevent this, he mustered the army of Parliament, and advanced to meet the Scots.

Cromwell wasted no time, and was over the Scottish border before the Scots were strong enough to prevent him. The two armies met at Dunbar where, although the Scots were beaten, their army was not destroyed. Very soon those who had escaped from the battle had rejoined King Charles, but they had no wish to fight another battle with Cromwell. They knew that his soldiers outnumbered them, and that their only chance was to avoid his army and march south into England.

Cromwell had moved his army to Perth, in the east, so Charles was able to march down the western side of Scotland to Carlisle.

His intention was to reach London and seize the crown before Cromwell could overtake him.

Cromwell quickly learned of the King's intention. Immediately he gave orders to his army and set off in pursuit.

King Charles did not march directly to London. He hoped by keeping on the western side of the country, where he believed he had many friends, to raise English volunteers for his army. But the English were tired of war, and very few joined him.

When Charles reached Worcester he had only about twelve thousand men, and Cromwell was close behind him with at least thirty thousand trained soldiers.

There was nothing Charles could do except turn and fight. Cromwell divided his forces into two halves, each of which was bigger than the King's whole army. Though Charles himself and his men fought bravely, they were caught between the two halves of Cromwell's army and beaten.

Charles escaped from the battle of Worcester, and by riding hard, he managed to get away from Cromwell's men. But his army was scattered, and he himself was being hunted by the Parliamentary soldiers. What was he to do?

With one or two others he reached the house of a family named Giffard. They were royalists and therefore on the King's side, but this meant that their house was all the more likely to be searched. It was therefore decided that King Charles must try to get to the coast and escape to France.

So that he could travel without Cromwell's soldiers recognising him, a disguise was obviously necessary. Some rough and badly worn peasants' clothes were soon found, and when his long hair had been cut, and with soot on his face and hands, the King of England looked like one of the poorest of his subjects.

It was just as well that Charles had disguised himself so thoroughly. The whole countryside was full of Cromwell's men searching for him, and he had many narrow escapes from capture.

With a faithful servant of the Giffards' named Richard Penderel, he set out on foot. But after wandering all night, they found that it was impossible to avoid the soldiers, and they returned to the house from which they had started.

Cromwell's men were all round them, and it seemed certain that the King would be caught. Every house was being searched, and there were soldiers on all the roads.

Then Richard Penderel had a good idea. Charles climbed high up into an oak tree, and though the soldiers actually searched the bushes beneath it, they never saw the King, who was looking down on them from the branches above.

Charles could not remain for ever disguised as a peasant, hiding in oak trees. It was necessary that he should get out of the country.

But how? The King was a very tall man, and even in disguise it was not possible to conceal his height. So it was decided that he must ride on horseback to Bristol, and there try to get a ship to take him to France.

In those days it was quite usual for young ladies to ride on a pillion seat behind the saddle of a manservant. Charles, riding alone, might be suspected, but dressed as a servant, with a young lady behind him, he might pass without notice.

So the King of England rode away for Bristol with a young lady named Mistress Lane behind him. And though in one village they rode right through a party of Cromwell's soldiers, they were never stopped or questioned.

Unable to find a suitable ship in Bristol, King Charles sailed from Brighton, which was then a small fishing village called Brighthelmstone, in the autumn of the year 1651.

For a time he remained in France, but Cromwell thought that this was too close to England. It would be easy for the King to cross twenty miles of the English Channel and again try to regain the crown.

So Cromwell persuaded the French King to send Charles away. First he went to Germany, and later he lived in Bruges or Brussels, but always he kept alive the hope that one day he would be able to return to England.

Charles was not able to live richly in kingly style. He was very poor, and afterwards he used to look back with amusement on the time when he even had to do his own cooking.

Meanwhile the country was being governed by Cromwell, and the joy and happiness of merry England came to a sudden end. Theatres were closed, and singing and dancing were forbidden. The maypoles, which used to be on every village green in the country, were cut down, and life became sad, dull, and monotonous.

One of the greatest Englishmen of all time has written: "To the mass of the nation the rule of Cromwell manifested itself in the form of numberless and miserable petty tyrannies, and thus became hated as no Government has ever been hated in England before or since".

One of those who realised that many people in England were weary of Cromwell and the Puritans, was a general called Monck. He had fought against Charles I, but now he realised that England could only be happy again under a King.

In the year 1658 Cromwell died, and Monck sent messengers secretly to Charles, to try to arrange for him to return.

Not everyone in England wanted to be ruled by a King again. The men who had been in power under Cromwell were of course against it.

General Monck knew that only a show of force would bring the doubtful people to his side, so he gathered an army in Scotland and marched to London.

There was no fighting. People were only too glad to welcome a change, and when Monck summoned a free Parliament there was general relief throughout the country.

Charles soon learned what was happening in England. He promised that if he became King, no one who had fought against him should suffer, and that he would always rule with the consent of Parliament.

So on a day in May, 1660, the flags fluttered and the cannon fired a royal salute, and the rightful King returned to his country, nine years after he had left it, a hunted fugitive.

The King's journey from Dover to London was a triumphal procession all the way. There had been no rejoicing in England for so long that it was as though a great flood of happiness had been suddenly released.

In London the narrow streets were crowded with men, women, and children, come to welcome the King. The cobbles were strewn with flowers, and every house was gay with flags. Bells were ringing and there were cheering crowds everywhere. The people of England felt themselves delivered from a nightmare.

And at night, sides of beef were roasted at great fires, and barrels of wine were broached in the streets. London had got a King again, and everyone was glad, except a few sour-faced Puritans who, we may be sure, were careful to keep out of the way.

But the man who was happiest of all was King Charles II. His wanderings were over.

Although the people were glad—in the words of a song which everyone was singing—to see "the King enjoy his own again", they took care to ensure that there should be no more fighting in England.

One way of doing this was to see to it that there was no large regular army which the King might use to force unpopular laws on the country. So the soldiers who had fought in the Civil War were paid off, and within a year all had returned to civil life.

An exception was however made in the case of one regiment. These were the soldiers who had marched with General Monck from Scotland, and who had played such a large part in bringing the King back to England.

This regiment remains to-day, the Coldstream Guards, so called because it was at the village of Coldstream that they crossed the River Tweed on their famous march to London.

England soon settled down to the life which the people had known before the Civil War. It is true that there was a war with the Dutch, but it was fought at sea, and ordinary men and women knew very little about it.

Unhappily, the new-found content did not last very long. A terrible visitation was on the way, about which they were soon to know a great deal. This was the plague of London.

It began in the rat-infested areas of the docks, but it rapidly spread throughout London. No one was safe. People avoided each other for fear of infection, and all public gatherings were forbidden.

For months the bells tolled, and men went out with carts through the streets calling "Bring out your dead". Door after door was marked with the cross, which showed that someone in the house had the plague.

By the end of the year, seventy thousand people in London had died.

The plague of London lasted for a year. Then the bells ceased to toll and people began to breathe freely again, until suddenly another disaster struck at London.

The old wooden houses, with their open hearths and twisted chimneys, were very liable to catch fire. When they did so, it was almost impossible to prevent the fire from spreading.

This is what happened on Sunday morning, September the 2nd, 1666. A baker's shop in a street called Pudding Lane caught fire. There was a strong wind and it had been a very hot, dry summer. Before noon hundreds of houses had been destroyed, and the fire was still spreading.

As soon as King Charles heard of the danger which threatened London, he left his Palace of Whitehall and went into the City, encouraging the fire fighters and directing and helping the people.

It was soon obvious that unless something drastic was done, London would be entirely destroyed. The streets were very narrow, and the houses were built of wood, very close together. When one house caught fire it was certain that the fire would spread to the next one.

So orders were given that whole streets were to be pulled down, or blown up with gunpowder, to make wide gaps across which the fire could not spread.

In those days there were no fire-engines to go dashing through the streets the moment a fire broke out. Hundreds of sailors were hurriedly brought from the ships on the Thames, and soon they were breaking down the wooden houses with axes and ropes. Others were fighting the fire by forming chains of men, passing leather buckets of water from one to another.

All their efforts had little effect, and by the time the fire had burnt itself out, a third of London was in ruins.

More than thirteen thousand houses and nearly a hundred churches, including St. Paul's Cathedral, were destroyed in the great fire. Hundreds of shops and warehouses, with all the goods which they contained, were burnt.

This meant that scores of thousands of people were homeless, and with nothing to eat. They had fled from the fire, with what little they could carry, to the fields outside London, and here they were living in tents, or in such huts as they could build with branches and turf.

As soon as the fire had burnt out, King Charles rode out to Moorfields to see what could be done to help these unfortunate people. Supplies of food were brought in from the surrounding country, and the homeless were soon billeted in the buildings which remained.

The fire of London did one good thing. It cleared the way for the building of a new London, with wider streets and stone buildings.

The plague of London and the great fire were not the only disasters which England suffered in the early years of the reign of Charles II.

At that time we were at war with Holland, and there were many fierce battles between the Dutch and English ships. Shortly before the outbreak of the fire in London, the two fleets had met in the English Channel, and the battle lasted four days. The cannonade was so fierce that the sound of it was heard in London, and finally the Dutch admiral, de Ruyter, won the battle, and the English ships retreated up the Thames.

Worse was to follow. The next year, whilst the English people were still weakened by the plague and the great fire, another Dutch admiral, de Witt, sailed up the river and broke through the great boom which guarded Chatham harbour. The English were taken by surprise, and de Witt not only burnt four of our ships, but towed away the great English ship of the line, the Royal Charles.

After the English ships had been burned by the Dutch, it was of course necessary to build more ships to replace them. King Charles at once turned to the task of creating a new Navy.

At this time there was an official at the Navy Office named Samuel Pepys. We know a great deal about him because he kept a very famous diary, in which he tells us how he and the King planned the new ships.

King Charles was a very able man. There was very little concerning the building and sailing of ships which he did not thoroughly understand, and Mr. Pepys was probably the best organiser the Navy has ever had. England was fortunate in having two such men working together.

The King and Mr. Pepys spent long hours over beautifully made models, some of which still exist to-day. Soon the ships were being built, and within three years England had a Navy again.

It was during the reign of Charles II, five years after the great fire, that something very extraordinary happened. The crown of England was stolen.

The crown jewels were kept then, as they are still kept to-day, strongly guarded in the Tower of London. There is probably nothing in the whole country more difficult to steal.

This did not prevent a man called Colonel Blood from deciding to try. He dressed himself as a clergyman and managed to become very friendly with the keeper of the crown jewels, whose name was Edwards. Mr. Edwards and his wife and daughter were completely deceived, and when the friendly clergyman said that he had a rich nephew who would like to marry the daughter, they were very pleased indeed.

So Colonel Blood brought his nephew to call on them and whilst they were there, asked Mr. Edwards to show them the Crown jewels. Then, suddenly, they seized him, tied him up, and made off with the crown.

Fortunately they were stopped before they got out of the Tower.

King Charles had been fortunate in finding Samuel Pepys to help him in rebuilding the Navy; he was equally fortunate in finding the right man to plan the rebuilding of London.

Christopher Wren was a professor of astronomy at Oxford, but Charles knew that he was also an architect of genius. So he sent for Wren and together they set to work to repair the damage caused by the great fire.

Wren prepared a plan which would have made London the finest city in the world, but it would have cost so much that it had to be abandoned. Only in the churches which he designed, and in the great cathedral, do we see what London might have been.

The Cathedral of St. Paul's is Wren's greatest work. For nine years he drew and altered plans for the building, always showing them to the King and discussing them with him. At last, in 1675, the first stone was laid.

It was not until thirty-five years later that the Cathedral was finished.

There is in London another famous building built by Christopher Wren. This is the Royal Hospital, Chelsea.

The Chelsea Hospital was founded by Charles II, but it is not what we to-day call a hospital. It is a home for old soldiers, and those who live in it wear a special uniform, a long red coat and a particular kind of black hat.

They are known as Chelsea Pensioners, and they can be seen going about London to-day, still wearing a uniform designed nearly three hundred years ago.

There is a story that Charles founded Chelsea Hospital because Nell Gwyn, a famous actress at that time, told the King that it was a shame to let old soldiers starve. Whether this story is true or not, the Hospital was not completed until 1692, seven years after the King's death.

It was such actions as this which made Charles popular with the people.

King Charles was interested in a great many things. He founded the Royal Society for the advancement of scientific knowledge, and had himself a chemical laboratory where he carried out many experiments.

At the same time, he was fond of open air sports. He was a good tennis player and a famous yachtsman, and as a horseman he was one of the finest in the country. This meant that he took a particular interest in the breeding of race-horses, and in racing itself.

At that time Newmarket was a small village. But the country round about it consisted of open downs, on which to exercise and race the horses of the King's stable.

Soon it became a place of importance, to which the King and his Court went for weeks at a time, two or three times a year. The interest which Charles took in racing resulted in English horses becoming some of the best in the world.

Although Charles was a popular King, liked by the people as a whole, this country was not always peaceful during his reign.

It was a time when there was much bitterness about religion. Though both were Christians, Protestants and Catholics belonged to different churches and hated each other.

King Charles's younger brother, James, was a Catholic. Charles was a Protestant. The Protestants wanted to make sure that James would never be King, and in order to prevent this happening, they pretended that the Catholics were plotting to kill Charles.

The Protestants were led by the Earl of Shaftesbury, and one night they swarmed into the courtyard of the Palace.

It was a very noisy, rough, and dangerous mob, but Charles went out on to the balcony to quieten them. James was afraid that in the excitement someone might shoot at the King, but Charles said, "Have no fear, James. No one will ever kill me to make you King".

It was during the reign of King Charles II that one of the most important documents in the history of English liberty was signed by the King.

This was called the "Habeas Corpus Act". These are words in the Latin language meaning "thou hast the body", and they referred to the person of anyone detained in prison, whose presence was required in a court of Law. What the Act really meant was that no person could henceforth be kept in prison without being brought before a court and charged with the offence for which he had been arrested.

This Act is still important to-day, but it was even more important in 1679, when it was first passed. In those days men were frequently thrown into prison because they had annoyed someone in authority, or because some enemy had accused them of crimes which they had not committed.

King Charles was dark and good-looking. What was much more important, he was a very friendly man. He liked to stroll about London or Newmarket without ceremony, and to talk to people rich and poor alike. As he was quick-witted and amusing, as well as clever, those with whom he talked never forgot their conversation with the King.

But what perhaps made him most popular was that he was gay. The people of England were so weary of the joyless life they had been forced to live under Cromwell, that a King who loved music and singing and dancing, and all gay and happy things, was certain to be liked.

That is why King Charles II was known as the Merry Monarch.

Series 561